CRYSTALLIZING CHILDREN'S DREAMS

by

Katherine Lee West

"How beautiful upon the mountains are the feet of him that bringeth good tidings, that publisheth peace . . ."

Isaiah 52:7

Published by:

AMATA GRAPHICS

17937 S.W. Kelok

Lake Oswego, Oregon 97034

ISBN: 931224-01-2

Printed by: Millcross Litho, Inc.
Typeset by: Alphabet Type Shop

i

My deep appreciation is extended to Jim McCully whose invaluable advice and fine editing skills transformed a ponderous text into a wisdain conversane.

Also my indebtedness to Elaine Douglas whose thoughtfulness made this work possible, Connie Horvat for her superb graphic assistance, Mother for her patience in proofreading, and Russ Califf who synthesized all materials into a unified whole.

Special and heartfelt thanks go to Portland's COMMUNITY SCHOOL and ST. MARY'S ACADEMY (especially Sister Margaret Link) in The Dalles for the wonderful cooperation extended to me in my work with their children.

The young dreamer/artisans whose pictures make this book such a special delight to behold are: Tim Reesman, cover design; Billy Humbert, butterfly insert; Rebecca Macnab, Raoul Hill, Joie De Vivre, Mary Lumsford, David Johnson, and Kase Limmeroth, chapter designs

The butterflies fluttering throughout come from Holly Powell, Chris McCormick, and Jennifer Ingebo.

This book is dedicated to all the children with whom I have worked. I shall always cherish their joy, their spontaneity, and their love for the playfulness and wisdom of dreams. What I have learned from them can never be found in book or in lecture, for it is the kind of knowledge that engraves itself in the heart.

TABLE OF CONTENTS

Joie De Vivre

Seven years ago I had a dream which to this day remains vivid. In the dream I am a teacher of young children. They are a wondrous group. Together we delight in classroom antics. It appears though that the antics serve a purpose, since learning is obviously in progress.

I am drawn in particular to one little girl. She is serious, yet playful, wise but still child-like. She tells me her name is Joie De Vivre which I know to be French for "joy of being". She is aptly named, for in her presence I feel a lightness and wonderment anchored in deep inner peace. Together we marvel, we dance, and we play.

My supervisor enters, and I share with her my elation in having Joie in the class. The supervisor looks at me strangely and remarks: "Oh yes, do give her your attention, for she is going blind."

At the time of the dream I was just commencing my work in interpretative studies in symbolic dream messages. It would have demanded one giant step to admit that most of the cast, scenery, and props portrayed on my nightly state were part and parcel of myself, quite another to actually internalize the message contained in each symbol.

I could acknowledge Joie as obviously the child within — but going blind? That was a message my ears chose not to hear. Besides, my academic career had just begun. There were classes to teach, papers to write, an image to build, a facade to maintain, "serious" work to be done. Joie was forgotten.

On occasional moments, the outer world dropped away. Then sand dollars applauded when I danced on the beach, and jelly-fish joked as I bowed body forward and looked at waves backwards between my legs. Moments treasured, yet moments measured, as I returned home to take up my more "adult" guise, completed, of course, by the most stylish of blinders.

But there comes a time when even chic goggles do blind, for my intuitive vision was becoming noticeably impaired. Such was difficult to acknowledge. Yet as I realized I must in order to live more wholistically, wonder of wonders, to my rescue came advisors of impeccable credentials. They visited me nightly and often imparted the most penetrating of advice. Some of what they said was difficult to put into practice. It involved taking risks, and I was still accustomed to the security of blinders which kept certain things hidden from view. Yet I knew growth into wholeness depended upon application of the wisdoms these authorities spoke. Gradually under their deft guidance, I found myself slowly commencing to feel more free and more integrated in all parts of my being.

After years of listening and putting their advice into practice (albeit often in the most fumbling of ways), my mentors informed me I was to take on a new role. In one of their nightly messages, they informed me I was to be given the responsibility for teaching teachers how to swim.

These advisors customarily speak in allegorical style. Over the years of communion I have come to learn that images of water or activities therein connected have to do with work at unconscious levels. That is a part of our psyche deep as the ocean, with unfathomable treasures for the one willing to dive deep. As such a dive is most safely undertaken through the medium of dreams, it appeared I would soon be teaching others how to delve into their own dream materials.

But who were the "teachers" so eager to dive? Can you guess? Aye, indeed. For you see, these talented advisors are slight-of-hand artists as well. They proceeded to materialize the children I had seen in the classroom in my dream of seven years ago. Defying the limitations of time and space, they whisked me from a nighttime premonition to a daylight reality.

There was a minor alteration: the children seemed collectively to be Joie De Vivre. They took to my diving instruction as though they were reawakening to dormant skills. No wonder the treasures they brought back from their dives were worthy of ransom! Before I knew it, they had become my instructors. Their "joie" and shared treasures provided a course of study I would wager to be unequalled in the most hallowed halls of learning.

And Joie De Vivre herself? Well, she came back in a vision awhile ago. She has worked through her blindness and, feeling more whole, says we are to form a partnership for the work to be done. At times that work will be playful, at times more serious. Such is the "joy of being". And as long as our vision remains clear, we too can swim to great depths, finding treasures to share.

Crystallizing Children's Dreams

 Eager and excited, countenance expressing wonderment, a little lady with eyes ever so bright could hardly wait to share her dream with us:

I am riding my tricycle down a street. I pedal past stores that have many pretty toys and things to play with in the windows. But I don't stop. I keep right on pedaling. I pass other little boys and girls playing, but I don't stop to be with them either. It seems I am just supposed to keep on going. Finally I come to the most beautiful house I have ever seen. It has a big yard and many pretty trees and flowers. It looks like two big balloons are floating over the house with strings attached to the roof. I get off my tricycle and walk closer so I can see them better. But as I do, I see they are not balloons at all. One is Jesus floating there and the other is his mother Mary. They are so peaceful and happy moving about gently. I feel very peaceful and happy too and want to stay there forever.

There is something exquisite about the fabric of children's dreams. Powerful though a dream may be, it still retains the graceful fragility of fine blown crystal. And the child poised between the worlds of inner and outer reality may well regard dreams as more viable messages than those which impinge from the waking modes of existence. But to share them with an adult is to share a priceless treasure. If the gift is received with less than empathic regard, not only is there danger of shattering the crystalline contours of the dream, but also an important filament of communion may be severed between adult and child.

In the world of the young, the dream is pictorially vivid, yet often simple in design, with fewer subplots than found in the adult dream. Frequently there is a picturesque fable-like quality which presents a tale with such naivete that one is caught by the yet uncluttered world of the child's inner psyche. Consider for example this dream of Lee's:

> There is a bed in my dream, and it has a lump in one corner of it. The grown-ups are very upset because they don't think a bump looks nice. They try to pound it out, but it doesn't go away. When they leave, I begin to talk to the lump. I tell it I am sorry the adults tried to change it and to make it go away. The bump talks to me too, and we become good friends. It's okay for there to be bumps and lumps; they are supposed to be here like we are. It is really nice when they become our friends.

One of the richest dimensions in listening to the dreams of the young is becoming aware of the abundance of imagery contained therein. One does not have to hear very many dreams before it becomes all too obvious that the child's unconscious contains a vast accumulation of the wondrous materials from which poetry, prose and painting are born. Within this creative realm parents and educators will find fertile ground as they come increasingly to encourage the child to celebrate the latent myth-making material.

It must be stressed, however, that the higher mental functions seldom enter into the child's nightly "dreamas". Unconscious content is, by-and-large, still immune to the interference of the forming personality. It seems absurd and potentially damaging to attempt formal dream analysis with children while their ego (the reality testing principle of the psyche) is delicate and still in process of formation.

In the adult, reality-testing and conscious development are more fully formed so that most of us may integrate unconscious materials if we choose. For example, I dream of myself in a television studio, preparing to take part in a talk-show. Everything seems in order with the exception of the lipstick which I am applying. It is a brazen ruby red, which in my waking state I would never think of wearing. I awaken and realize that to appear on a television program for which I am scheduled next week would be inappropriate. The dream leads me to question my motive for agreeing to appear. I realize I am overly concerned with public image, and since I do not yet have resource materials to share with the viewing audience, an appearance at this point of time would be unwise. I cancel the appearance.

A grown person concerned with wholistic functioning will attend to such messages and work toward integrating those disparate parts of self revealed by the psyche through the medium of dreams. However, that same process in the child might foster a morbid self-interest or perhaps force him/her into a fantasy world far removed from reality. In the child, unconscious material can be overwhelming if there is an attempt to be analytical about its imagery. For this reason, the inner processes must be externalized if the child is to gain insight or mastery over them. This is done by allowing the child to distance him/herself from dream materials, to see them as something external. In so doing, one learns to take charge of them in a more integrative fashion. Working with dreams creatively facilitates this process.

However these crystalline dreams are shared and portrayed, guidance is needed from one who has developed some measure of artistry with his/her own nightly productions. If we are to understand and facilitate communion with the inner world of the child, we must first be in close touch with our own. Over the years, both parents and educators have been participants in my classes in dream interpretation. They are aware that, in order to legitimately encourage their children to work with dreams, they must themselves have gained some expertise with their own. Classes and workshops are becoming increasingly available in most urban centers; in addition there are several good books and periodicals in circulation. But what is far more important than any book or class is experience with one's own dreams. The best place to begin with dreams is always with your own, and that entails the willingness to begin exactly where you are — even if that means endeavoring for the first time to recall a dream.

It may well be you already have the skills for remembering and retaining dreams. If not, following the guidelines for children will undoubtedly do the trick. Once such skills are mastered, it is wise to ask what it is we want to accomplish in working with dreams. The answer will determine the form of encounter undertaken.

Many adults are drawn to serious interpretative work. That is to say, they wish to more fully integrate the physical, emotional, mental, and spiritual aspects of their being. Dreams address each of these areas. Although the form of encounter is of a creative intuitive nature, the goal is serious, for it has to do with integrative psychological work. Moreover, dreams are increasingly recognized as a practical way of receiving information about those portions of self which we may have disowned, repressed or projected upon others. They also serve as sources of information about unfamiliar parts of ourselves. For integrating polarities of oneself, this kind of data can be a necessary and critical part of the journey toward wholeness and actualization. Forms such as "gestalt" and "circumambulation"[1] are designed to enable a person to intuit the symbolic meaning of these dream messages.

These more serious approaches tend to be the primary fashion in which adepts work with dreams, but the creative approach to dream cracking must be given equal weight in its potential for facilitating new growth. Ostensibly this book is written for children; yet any adult who dances the dream, gives it poetic form, sculpts it or paints it in pastels is sure to find an equally powerful personal meaning contained in its message.

There is a third way which stands midway between these two; that of honoring the dream simply in the spirit of play. Dreams themselves are highly playful. They pun, they plot, they entertain. Listen to anyone relate a dream. S/he is in fact giving a reading from a highly ingenious dramatization. In workshops we often commence by telling one of our dreams, sometimes after painting it on paper. By the time of the last sharing, the atmosphere is charged with gaiety, conviviality, laughter, and wonderment. This is the beauty of playing with what is already so play-full. Play is truly a creative unfoldment of our personal world, and when we open to encounter with what are known to be playful offshoots of psychic dialogue, the result is a lightness and a joy which are valid as ends in themselves.

Play creates not so much in terms of what it "produces" but in terms of what it "sees". Playing with a dream may not be the pinacle of creativity, but it does serve as a foundation for imaginative perception, and such is basic to the growth of creativity in life. Since play appears to be one primary way by which human beings continue to open themselves to fresh insight and creative development, the simple act of honoring the dream or sharing it with another may give a special form of completion to it. Later one may wish to go back to it and work with it in a more serious or revealing way.

As you become more familiar with the world of your own dreams, you grow in appreciation of a multitude of ways of working with your own group of children. Not that I have any illusions about "teaching" dreams. As if anyone can "teach" to another! But we can both affirm and lead forth that which is quite poised and on the brink of the child's inner world, waiting for us to stretch forth our arms. From that point on, it is a matter of growing together into a dimension that is indeed crystalline, yet intensely strong in its bonding nature and ability to crystallize the special kinds of relationships that result from sharing inner depths.

Celebrating the Dream

It was my first day working with children and their dreams. A group of six-year-olds had assembled, and we were seated in a circle on the floor getting acquainted. I had barely begun talking about dreams when Shiloh, a rambunctious young fellow in cowboy boots said: "You know what the best way is to remember your dreams?"

Not knowing I was about to be upstaged, I replied: "What do you think it is?"

He responded: "Dream chains of course, cuz if you sleep with them the right way under your pillow, you get all the dreams you want!"

"Who had come to teach dreams to whom?" I wondered to myself and gladly gave him the floor for further exposition.

It appeared the chains usually were of special metals and the hand must be placed just so under the pillow, resting lightly on the chain itself. The children were wide-eyed. This young man was a ringleader and the authority on many subjects, but his peers had never heard him speak to this matter. Enthusiasm was high as was their sense of wonderment. It was obvious if we were to become dreamers of first rank, we must find a way to construct fragile structures in most cases is alive and healthy; one can see it in the child's eyes when the subject of dreams is presented. These children may wish to remain on the periphery until intuition tells them it is safe to venture into actual encounter. If so, fine and well. Patience and understanding are our most trusty allies when it comes to entering into encounter with the child's inner world.

Often a more studied approach is the key to enabling the child to feel on secure ground. Rather than to commence with dream diaries and murals for the portrayal of their content, one instead moves more gently, using a time-honored circuitous approach. This has to do with looking at dreams more objectively. Later the child can be encouraged to work in more subjective and personalized ways. Such can be handled in a variety of fashions.

There are some in the reading audience who will be comfortable in allowing the child to make the initial explorations (older children), serving as a resource person for that which ensues once curiosity is aroused. With younger children, one can read aloud stories and anecdotes on dreams for a curtain raiser. However, I can guarantee it will not be long before the children themselves have upstaged the books' cast of characters with their own eager sharings.

I enjoy presenting some of the fascinating lore about dreams as we begin to warm up to the topic. Eight-year-olds are entranced by the fact Robert Louis Stevenson wrote portions of TREASURE ISLAND and DR. JEKYLL AND MR. HYDE from his dreams, that Elias Howe invented a crucial part of the sewing machine from his, and that Beethoven heard intricate musical scores as he slept and dreamed.

Sometimes the catalyst in opening a group comes from my sharing a dream or reading from my own dream diary. There are children who are literally amazed that an adult takes dream life so seriously, much less has dreams often much like their own.

I also find children like to discuss among themselves what they think dreams are all about, from whence they come and what value they serve. The caution here would be such a discussion becoming somewhat rhetorical. I prefer to use a more playful opener which paves the way for creative encounter with the these most special of chains. That took dialogue and a bit of brainstorming, but with Shiloh's approval, we decided we could fashion our own chains out of paperclips, painting them in special hues. Once completed it took a rite of incantation to christen them "dream chains", but they then met with Shiloh's approval. Harmony was the only dissenter. She was not so easily convinced that dream chains would guide her so effortlessly into her dreams. She decided she would sleep with her dream chain on alternative evenings. If she had better recall on nights when using her chain, she would know it to be a viable tool; if the reverse occurred, she would rely on her own inner counsel. I found myself speculating what the scientific method had to teach her at age six!

A rather innovative approach for the celebration of the dream. Yet one I suspect which could be equalled by other imaginative youngsters who listen to inner inspiration would we but ask. And whether it is dream chains or herb pillows, the intent is the same: to heighten the appreciation for the nightly visitations, at the same time imparting a technique which will facilitate recall of the events.

With children, this is best done in the spirit of celebration. If dream work appears ponderous or academic, you have lost your audience before the curtain goes up. A celebration of this nature may be a completely new experience for those who wish to open and share their inner world. Consequently, it is wise to first discern how the potential celebrants regard the subject matter which is to be staged.

Some youngsters will need only the most cursory of invitations to immediately join in the dance. It is almost as though they were poised and waiting for such an overture, so tumultuously do the ensuing sharings pour forth. These are the children who either through their own intuitive insights or environmental encouragings have retained the wonderment which arises from being in rapport with nightly murmurings.

Others may seem less exuberant. Perchance they harbor trepidations over fearsome dreams with which they have never been encouraged to come to grips. Or perhaps there was a time when that crystalline fabric was shattered in the fumbling hands wherein the dreams were entrusted. Yet the desire to rebuild the dreams. I have found when introducing dreams in this fashion, the children are intrigued and delighted, for they are self-defining what their nightly experiences are about and are then desirous to work more intimately with them.

"Metamorphosis" is a specialized form of word definition. It can be used equally well with concepts or symbols be they simple or complex. Since it is much more playfully creative than rationally academic, kindergarten age through senior citizens thoroughly enjoy its challenge. The following is a metamorphic definition of "dreams". But you might wish to pause first and take a deep breath. Better yet, breathe in deeply and read it aloud to gain a real feeling for the essence of what is at hand. Wink as you wince, for 'tis important to have the amplification reverberate with verve and delight:

Playfict dreams? Nay! Saneful elakie wisdains. Estasy in bevilish inakook conversane. Freudful approach is sleepish and fantaless. In reality, dreams are psyckoo and fulfoo of comtion. Moreover, they are E.S.Pable ishdoms of wishlish estasy. Conversare in foofor psyckoo makes for illality in psychowere playness!

As you can see, metamorphosis is a technique which couples playful merriment with probing pronouncements. Give the definition a bit of time to commence resonating, and you may well find those newly created words render a definition bordering on the profound.

The technique is quite simple: begin by taking a word, concept or symbol. In the manner of free association, give air to any positive images that appear. In gatherings we speak them out quickly, each association triggering others. Soon fifteen or twenty images fill the board. Then the exercise is repeated. But this time we may focus on the extreme of the word, its opposite or negative aspects of it. Again, a second list forms. Now for the "metamorphosis". Words from the two lists are combined, but only parts or syllables of respective words such that a whole new word and meaning are effected.

As this is a marvelous exercise in creative writing, one morning before composing poetry from our dreams, Elmira, Mary, Howard, Fran and myself undertook to metamorphosize the word "dream". What follow are our two lists and then the results of combining words from both:

Positive Associations

Sleep	Soul
Awareness	Comfortable
Wisdom	Conversation
Weightlessness	Playful
Communion	Relaxation
E.S.P.	Instructional

Far Out Associations

Unbelievable	Make-believe
Weird	Fiction
Foolish	Kookie
Freudian	Illogical
Senseless	Insane
Psyche	Fantasy

New Combinations

Fantaless	Saneful	Sleepish	Freudful
Illality	Playness	Psychowhere	Munish
Elakie	Inakook	Bevilish	Conversane
Estasy	Psyckoo	Playfict	Comtion
Fortane	Weightable	Ishdom	Senseness
E.S.Pable	Wisdain	Wishlish	Laylogical
Fullfoo	Lessax	Foofor	Espane

We now had a whole list of new words from which to construct a definition of dreams. The task was to fit together combinations using a minimum of nouns, verbs, articles and prepositions such that a "saneful" message would appear. Any and all produced could vie with my opener. Consider for example Elmira's:

My dreams show a psychowhere and psychoo of my sleepish senseness. A weightable fantaless inakook will lead me to Freudful estasy with no espane. No lessax need I wishlish foofor. Illality is playfict, fortane smiles in wisdain and saneful laylogical dreams!

The variations are as infinite as is the makeup of the group. The air tingles with creative virtuosity — not just from the conductor but from each and every musician. For truly this is music; it is the rhyme and rhythm that surface when the reasoning mind is set aside, allowing the wellsprings of creativity to inakook in wisdain estasies. And wonder of wonders, in the process we have come to embrace the dream. There is real insight in such definitions; they are far from meaningless jabberwocky. Once I metamorphosize a word, it takes on a whole new aura, for I now have taken it inside and have fully become it. The concept is really mine, not just what someone "out there" has told me about it.

What a difference both in affect and effect between this sort of exercise and merely asking the child in rhetorical fashion: "What is a dream?" And how much more delightful to then go on to draw, sculpt, paint or put into poetry those sleepish conversanes after having created one's very own definition of munish, saneful psyckoos. In fact, one or two words from the definition may become the personal slogan for any dream play that is to follow. I will stand and fall with my psychowhere conversanes while Elmira courts her illality playficts.

I often wonder if dreams have been neglected because although they occur within us, we persist in looking at them from outside of ourselves. We attempt to reason them out or go to great lengths to read what others claim they are all about. Children become bored by either of those processes, and perhaps we need to take our cue from them. Little ones seem to intuit that the dream is dancing on that innermost stage of the psyche, issuing nightly invitations to embrace its beat. That means throwing reason to the wind and imaginatively becoming a co-creator of the dance. True, it may take a psyckoo to conversane in such fashion, but if such estasy is deemed fullfoo, then our dream wisdains are rendered senseness. PSYCKOOS UNITE! There is a great group. They are mostly under age; a bevilish bunch. Laylogical perhaps, but saneful in weightable ways.

An interesting side-note is this: I have had children who loved their work with dreams but would come in crestfallen when others of their peer group made fun of what they were doing and implied dreams were nonsense. However, when we start off metamorphosizing dreams, the youngsters seem to be convinced this is an area of joyful legitimacy. Others may laugh, scoff or belittle, but the children don't mind. They seem to realize their tauntors are fantaless foofors and return the ridicule with compassionate smiles.

Whatever technique you draw upon, once you are assured of a captive audience, there is one ground rule I strongly recommend following: the keeping of a dream diary.

Dream diaries are a chronicle of a child's very own communications which can be shared, treasured and marveled over in the months to come. They are the codification of dreams in written form and are a source of endless fascination to most children. I remember the proud faces of a six-year-old class the day they first brought back their dream journals with the first recorded dreams. Any one of them could have been one of the magi, bearing a priceless treasure. On this momentous occasion, each was asked to read the dream aloud in our sharing session, speaking it into my tape recorder so they could later hear themselves in their first sharing.

And who was it, pray tell, that said "Johnny can't read?" Two in the group ostensibly could not read — at least not the first grade materials they had been assigned. But their own dream? Quite another matter! For several, a cooperative parent had written the dream in the diary itself, but in such a way that they captured for the most part the child's exact wording. Hence with only minimal help, each read aloud in the fashion of a polished performer. I felt myself wanting to send out a resounding call to every primary teacher who had ever been witness to young ones struggling in that hesitating, halting fashion so painful to slow readers. How totally different when reading material no longer was strangely foreign, but rather had emerged from the wellsprings of one's own inner being.

Any educator who has revered Sylvia Ashton Warner's small treasure TEACHER[2] knows well the rewards of teaching reading via the children's own writings. Here is a new application of an old principle which works wonders with very young children. Although I have not used the technique with those under six, I suspect many four-year-olds would respond in the same fashion.

With the younger age group, parental cooperation seems to be the key in enabling dream work to become particularly meaningful. Since it would be difficult if not impossible for most to write down their own dreams, help from the parent is a must. When this happens, a rich form of communication is possible between parent and child, which further legitimizes sharing of the inner world experiences.

Older children, not as dependent upon parental aid, do remarkably well left to their own design. I have found, however, that any interest and encouragement shown by the parent makes the dream encounters seem all the more worthwhile to the child. In addition, recall is enhanced and intuitive insights deepened.

What actually is a dream diary? Why such an emphasis on the need for a child to keep one? First of all, children, especially the younger ones, are masters and mistresses of the world of fantasy. All too often a teacher sets aside part of a morning's sharing session for dreams, only to discover that children are not telling dreams so much as tales of make-believe, intertwined with movie plots and television scripts. I know of educators who have ceased trying to honor the dream because it took such a secondary place to fantasy games. Of course, I find fantasy a very rich subject and would never wish to discourage its use when being adaptively applied. (I am not speaking here of the type of fantasy trips which serve as escapism when a child's anxiety level is high.) But if time is to be set aside for working with dreams, then fantasy must become peripheral. Later, the two may be blended.

Fantasizing endings for one another's dreams can be a delightful exercise which children seem to love, and I might add, an exercise at which they seem particularly adept. Also, some fantasizing may be honored when dream sharings are commencing — particularly for those children who have not brought a dream with them. For some, it may well be that sharing a fantasy is a safer way to begin than the telling of a personal dream. However, I have found that once encounters begin with actual dreams, wherein they are treated with great respect, honor and delight, there is less and less reliance on fantasy.

Diaries also provide a means for the child to give a more exact accounting of the dream. Memory is fallible even at age seven. Details drop out quickly, and even though I have found young ones more adept at dream recollection than adults, they, too, have to reckon with the factors of interference.

In the final analysis, diaries are a codified way of sharing special parts of our experience, even if the sole recipient is the dreamer him/herself. My own dream diary is a never-ending source of wonderment for me and also an excellent reference for inspiration. If I were involved in creative writing classes, I know where I would go for my materials. When a class is involved with their dreams, a writing instructor seldom confronts the obstinate situation of: "I don't have anything to write about."

Diaries can be made of a variety of materials. Usually I gather together 8½ x 11 construction paper in a myriad of colors. From there on out, it is a matter of personal preference. It may take the form of crayons, paints, or scissors for making cutouts. I also have handy a punch, eyelets and a supply of lined notebook paper. I have my own dream diary with me, or more exactly a second one which I have fashioned much like the children do theirs out of colored paper. Special dreams have been recorded in this diary — usually those that have reference to the work I am doing with the children. These are the ones I read when it feels right to share my own as a point of reference.

The covers of the children's dream diaries never cease to fascinate me. There are those who opt for a symbol or picture from some particularly vivid dream; others seem to know intuitively what should be portrayed on their cover. There is usually a great deal of pride in the finished product and an eagerness to begin recording.

With a group of six year olds, I prepare a mimeographed sheet to take home with them in their dream diaries. It explains what we are going to attempt to do with dreams and asks for parental help in aiding the child to record what comes through at night in his/her special journal. I also suggest selected references in the dream literature, in case parents themselves might like to understand more about the nature of this work.

Certainly encouraging family participation is important. Many readers will be parents themselves and already committed to sharing dream experiences within the family setting. When such is the case, interaction will go beyond merely helping the younger children record dream remembrances in a journal or encouraging older ones to do so of their own accord. Most likely there will be a desire to actually share dreams together as respective family members begin to honor this rich dimension of inner experience.

It is fascinating to compare cultural notes on the Senoi Indians of the Malay Peninsula. This group of tribespeople has fashioned an entire way of life about their dreams. Each morning the family, while gathered together for breakfast, shares dreams of the past night. They begin with the youngest, who receives both praise and encouragement for what s/he has to offer. Such mastery have these people gained over the dream process itself that children are given suggestions regarding action they may wish to take in future dreams. Later in the morning, the adults group together in the form of a tribal council, at which time questions regarding the government and welfare of the tribe are considered, drawing on wisdom garnered from their dreams.

This particular culture is currently of vital interest to western psychologists and anthropologists because they are an amazingly healthy and autonomous group. For the past three hundred years they have experienced virtually no violent aggression, insanity or armed conflict. About one-quarter of their waking hours is spent in farming and hunting wherein simple, efficient methods are employed. The rest of the time they are busily engaged in developing gifts and symbols shown to them in their dreams. They teach one another songs, dances, poetry, and stories received from their dreams and prepare for evening celebrations by making costumes decorated with dream symbols.

Variations on this kind of interaction have been recorded by those who study our own American Indian tribes. The Iroquois believed in the sovereign power of the dream and contended that visitations from on high took place in dreams. It was believed that dreams revealed hidden wishes of the soul, and that family members and relatives could help interpret. Therefore an important part of an extended families' interaction pattern was that of listening to one another's dreams and endeavoring to give by acts, dances or special gifts that which the soul of a loved one required for continued good health.

Whether we study the Senoi, the Iroquois, or other of the ancient cultures, what never fails to manifest is a very closely knit family structure. It may well be that family therapists, child psychologists and parents themselves could gain immeasurably by extrapolating from such cross-cultural studies.

It is gratifying to hear parents in classes speak about the changes within the family where dream-sharing has become a part of the interaction pattern. Often it demands a real commitment to make time for a practice so foreign to a culture which tends to reinforce only external kinds of sharing. But bonds created are strong and meaningful. One can only guess at the potential psychological problems avoided by engaging in this exchange. The models provided by cultures such as the Senoi are powerful directives pointing to enhanced health and well being both interpersonally and intrapersonally. Only the family who undertakes such a venture can truly gauge its effctiveness; knowledge can never become wisdom until it is applied.

How does one set the stage for the celebration of the dream? Although children do not need quite the priming as do adults who profess minimal dream recall, some pointers may be helpful. Autosuggestion is among the best: simply telling myself before falling asleep that I can and will recall a dream upon awakening gives a mental set conducive to remembering. Talking about dreams before bedtime, reading about them or sharing dream experiences also enhances mental set. We remember what we choose to pay attention to. Any act which brings the dream to the forefront of awareness will be conducive to dream recall.

For children, dreams are vivid, and they tend not to lose them as quickly as do adults. Perhaps when they awaken they do not immediately begin the rehearsals and head chatter of the adult, or at least not to the same degree. Therefore, there is not so much interference which tends to mediate against recall. It is still wise, however, to record or share the dream as close to the time of its occurrence as possible. A quiet time spent together in dream sharing is a special way of opening the day and sets a smoother rhythm than does a too hasty breakfast and mad dash for the school bus. Again, this takes a strong commitment; inevitably it means a drastic alteration in schedule. It might be more workable for some to instigate such a plan first on weekends and then allow it to pick up its own momentum.

In one class we made small dream pillows. These contain a combination of herbs which help facilitate recall in that they appear to enhance the vividness of the dreams themselves.[3] The herbs are to be blended in the following combination:

1 part	Barberry Root
2 parts	Raw Dandelion Root
1 part	Lemon Verbena
1 part	Lemon Grass
1 part	Mistletoe
2 parts	Eucalyptus

We used colorful cotton material in finished size of 3" by 4". Needless to say, the group learned a lot about herbs that day as well as stitchery! Some of the children found the pillows helpful; others reported they tossed and turned too much to keep them on their larger pillows. One young man, much too sophisticated to consider dream work legitimate up to this point, confided that his mother had already made him a special dream pillow of velvet embroidered with the moon and the stars. He treasured it very much but apparently felt his ten-year-old peer group would not think it very masculine; hence he slept with it only on special occasions. Whether he began to use it on a more regular basis after that session I do not know, but he did enter into sharing from that time onward.

Children themselves have very clear and original ideas about how they can facilitate their own dream recall. I would advise seeking their insights on the matter for more innovative twists. In any case, the reader will not have to exert him/herself overly to commence the celebration. In most cases, the stage lights will be on and the orchestra tuned. As I see it, it is just a matter really of sage character direction because the scripts themselves will bring down the house. Let's turn then to a consideration of how the scripts may be best presented so the talents of the dreamer may be given full view — not out of concern for the audience, but for the enhanced growth of the one choosing to share the script.

Creative Applications

As the sharing session began, Carmen had no interest in verbalizing her dream. Rather, she headed directly to the paints and paper set out on the table. The next few minutes were busy ones as she selected colors with great care, contemplated how best to utilize them in portraying her dream, and then proceeded with her artistic rendition. The creation completed, she eagerly awaited the reassembling of our group. No words were needed to describe her picture as she proudly displayed it to our view. It was a wondrous rainbow resplendent with colors galore. We took a few moments simply to experience it. Then, with voice as soft as her eyes, Carmen shared with us how this rainbow had appeared in her dream and what it meant to her. The moment was a very special one — not only for Carmen but for each one of us so honored by the glimpse into her inner world. Preparing to move on to Andrew's charcoal sketch, I noticed a splash of color on the backside of Carmen's picture. I inquired if she would also tell us about that. She looked at me almost in surprise and replied rather gently as though to remind me of a world I had forgotten: "Why, it is the backside of my rainbow, of course."

Is it any wonder that encouraging children to express creatively what comes to them in dreams is not only the most plausible but also a most joyful way of rendering their nightly word pictures? Dreams provide a never-ending source of creative expression, whether in poetry, pottery or paint. There is a verse in the Talmud that says the dream is its own interpretation. One might speculate that the Talmud implies creative expression, so that interpretation might stand strong and free.

We have entered an era where creative self-expression is once again encouraged, both in the home and in school. We are now seeing the counterface of an educational process too long devoted to instruction and programming. Instead of desensitizing persons to their own inner life, thankfully we are now seeing the child encouraged to remain in contact with realms of his/her own consciousness other than the purely rational and factual. The young person is encouraged to discover and enact his/her own unique forms of spiritual or creative expression.

There was a time when artistic manifestation was socially acceptable in proportion to its capacity to proffer fame or financial support. Otherwise, individuals tended to relegate creative inclination to status of "hobby" and tolerated it in the more bohemian element. However, in general, it was not accepted as a viable means of personal growth for the populace as a whole. As the culture enters a period of re-examination and a growing sensitivity to the need for developing an inner life to balance the outer, our views on the place of creative expression are rapidly changing.

Humans have always looked to the arts to symbolize, explore and give form to that which otherwise remains inexpressible. As if words could capture the grandeur of Wagner's compositions or the effervescent quality of a landscape drawn from the luminous level of a child's dream. Many now acknowledge artistic expression as a unique means of extending one's own personal selfhood inward, beyond the limits of time and space. As such, it is a means for self teaching and expanding one's own consciousness.

Creative expression can be seen as a form of yoga — yoga in its original meaning of "union" — union of body, soul and spirit. Not only is intense concentration required of the one who creates, but the forthcoming symbols, whether word pictures or clay figurines, offer very real messages from a deeper identity. In the very act of creating, the outer self becomes a receptive surface to be moulded by that which appears from within, teaching from the inside out. Socrates found the didactic method the only true one for learning; creative expression can be seen as an aspect of that mode of self education. What we create when we take brush, crayon or pen in hand is truly ourselves; we are involved with our own education for greater personhood.

In her book: CENTERING IN POTTERY, POETRY AND THE PERSON[4], M.C. Richards shares the story of a potter in ancient China: A nobleman riding through a village sees a potter at work. He stops to view the pots and finds them extraordinarily beautiful. He inquires of the potter how he is able to execute such grace, such strength, yet with such delicacy of design. The potter replies: "Oh, you are looking at merely the outward shape; what I am forming lies within. The only thing I am interested in is what remains after the pot has been broken."

This, then, is the act of creation. It is not merely the pot, the picture, the poem that we are forming; it is ourselves. The medium we select can encase only a portion of the spirit which inspires the production. While the light that dwells within will manifest itself through such a medium if we choose to give it reign, ultimately the medium is but the vehicle for honoring that place from whence the message arises.

In FESTIVALS IN THE NEW AGE[5], David Spangler speaks of the "inner festival" where all is brought to perfection and wholeness. He notes how in the past, individuals sought strengths which might enable them to gain mastery of their world. Lacking in contemporary society has been a means of familiarizing of self with those strengths which would enable us not so much to conquer but to blend with our world. For we are not the master of Nature, but rather an organic part of her, infilled by her energies. As we learn to affirm our rhythms, we awaken increasingly to that festival within; the celebration of peace, trust, love, wisdom, and light which manifests in co-creation with Nature.

Awakening to the dream can be awakening to spontaneous festivals staged every night, more entrancing than those artificially staged during special seasons of the year. Rather than remain passive spectators, in our own dream festivals we design the costumes, settings, events, and plot. All these can be brought from the dream and shared through a medium of one's own choosing.

Let's look at some of the choices open to the celebration of a child's dreams.

Whenever possible, I encourage a variety of materials be made available to the child. The images surfacing from different dreams lend themselves to various media. Dreams are such a rich source of inspiration, it may even be that the child never before drawn to poetry will find in that form a plenitude of emerging images from which to select. So many possibilities exist in the creative domain. Let me suggest just a few for starters. The reader undoubtedly can and will add others.

Crayons, Paints and Other Colors:

These are perhaps the most popular media for giving expression to the dream. What tends to surface first is the action, the theme or the mood of the dream. It makes no difference whether the portrayal is an exact replication or a more abstract rendering. The overriding concern is that the children be allowed to make drawings satisfying first to themselves.

The value of the "work" is proportionate to its release of creative power. Given a sincere attempt to express one's best, it is imperative that we accept and value it as such. Under the direction of an overly helpful guide, a "pretty" picture may emerge or one with skilled execution of design, but such are of no real value compared to a painting which gives direct expression to the child's creative powers. Adult ideas have often been known to improve the quality of the product, but the price is high: possible loss of the child's individual expression. More than ever, we need to grow beyond material values which prize the product rather than creative growth.

There have been times when I have chosen to reject a hasty scribble of a surrogate dream image, but the rejection was directed to the spirit behind the act. Never could I criticize an awkwardly expressed design which I know to be lovingly done. To do so would be to destroy the spirit for the letter.

Customarily after the paintings or drawings have been completed, we reassemble as a group to share our creations and the dream which brought them forth. Merely to display such renderings would be to lose a precious aspect of the dream. The sharing time elicits much joy and wonderment on the part of the group; one is witness to the profound respect with which others treat these messages from the inner world. It is a marvelous way of evoking appreciation of that vast and rich inner territory.

Sometimes we come back together and place our pictures all together in the middle of the floor. Marilyn takes one, Eddy another, Ben the third and so on. After a few minutes of quiet reflection time, we regroup our energies. Kimberly now has a story to share about Andrew's dream drawing. Andrew sits in rapt attention with his dream becoming all the more special as seen through Kimberly's eyes. The degree of originality the storyteller brings to the dream of another is fascinating; but even more amazing is how often the storyteller speaks to a theme contained within the original dream. This particular technique seems to foster both a closeness and a camaraderie among the children; further, it enhances empathy and intuitive insight. As can be seen, we are coupling storytelling with artistic expression, personalized by the dream. Little wonder that it becomes such a meaningful encounter for those involved.

Storytelling:

There are probably a dozen variations possible on the above storytelling theme. There is no reason why the dream must first be artistically expressed. Much will depend upon the age of the child; however, an artistic rendering does help the young ones focus more on the dream than a strict verbal rendition. More details seem to be remembered in this way as well. Such visual aids serve, too, as attention holders when a group comes together to dialogue.

One day we made a dream story book as a means of exploring our own variation on storytelling. I purchased a large paper scrapbook and covered the front and back with sheets of colored construction paper. Entitled "OUR DREAM STORY BOOK", the rest of the cover was marked off in boxes, one for each child. As the dreams for the day were shared from dream diaries, each child was asked to select from that dream a scene or symbol to portray on his/her portion of the cover. At the close of the sharing session, we then had six quite different and unique representations. Our task was then to make up our own group story wherein we could interweave all six of the frames.

The assignment would have challenged the imagination of J.R. Tolkien himself. Chris had drawn his chum Chard who had appeared in his dream garbed in a dress. Harmony had a magic woman who could create matter by an act of sheer mind power. Malea reproduced pet snakes who in her dream slithered in and out of her house. A special sort of swimming pool designed just for children was Shiloh's dream contribution. Vasu gave form to a gigantic claw rising up out of water, and Carmen drew her classmates who had been given wings and could fly to the aid of others in distress.

I wrote as the children conferred and dictated. It turned out to be an exercise involving cooperation, imagination, tolerance for the views of others and compromise, all underscored by great hilarity and delight. Rules of grammar were sacrificed to originality. Later on I had visions of the story being used to inculcate principles of sentence structure through group revision and editing (perhaps a more appropriate exercise for older audiences). Why on earth should dream work not become inter-disciplinarian? As it was, the dream story book replaced in terms of popularity its more polished counterparts on the storybook shelf!

Yet another variation is that of mingling fantasy with dream sharing. In this method, a child first shares a dream with the group. We all then become very quiet and still and the children are encouraged to go inside themselves so as to communicate with their very own fountain of imagination and fantasy. They can either pick up where the dream left off, or take some portion of it which was of special interest and follow it up with their own story line.

When the quiet time is up, we then share what came into our minds. This is a particularly fine way for honoring the dream itself. Children who present what they term as a "dumb dream" are amazed to see the impetus it provides for others to spin off creative insights. Actually, this is a group variation on a technique known as "active imagination". In active imagination an individual becomes very quiet, and after replaying the dream, allows imagination to then take it to wherever it may wish to go. From such ventures come personal insights, as well as poetry and prose. Such can come from children fantasizing about their own or another's dream.

Another idea is that after the fantasy time is over, rather than describe what has been seen, encourage the children to draw what they see. Roger was a tough little fellow who didn't like sharing fantasy trips because they were not a manly exercise. But how he did love to wield pastels. It did not at all seem a breach of masculinity to draw what he saw in his imagination; he was comfortable in his role of artist and had no hesitations about sharing his production when in that form!

Prose and Poetry:

Early in my dream work with children, I ferreted through what I could find in the literature that might give me aid and insight. One of the first resources I came across was Kenneth Koch's small treasure: WISHES, LIES AND DREAMS — TEACHING POETRY TO CHILDREN[6]. Koch, like so many literature teachers was aware that at early ages, children already had blocks when it came to writing and produced lifeless stereotypes, written perhaps in "good form" but sadly lacking in originality. Fortunately Koch was aware also of the power children have to perceive the world in fresh and beautiful ways. He felt that the desire to express that vision was inherent and could be used as a strong creative and educational force. Seeking ways to encourage and amplify such vision, he came to draw upon dreams, as well as wishes and lies, as a source of poetic inspiration. Dreams in particular seemed an appropriate way to enable children to become aware of their unconscious experiences. Once in touch with those experiences, only a small step is required to bring them forth into poetic rendition. A dream haiku? Why not? Certainly one is more simply aware in a dream, and the very awareness of that experience lends itself beautifully to the stylized Oriental form. Iambic pentameter? Not so difficult when one is in touch with the rhythms of the dream. The free verse contained in Koch's book is a joy to behold, clear evidence that his vision was a valid one — that children can and do see the world in its intricate yet pristine splendor and are able to extract teachings from a myriad of levels.

Lee was eager to attempt free form poetry with a dream encounter although staunchly disclaiming any poetic inclinations. The result was as philosophic as it was poetic:

> An elephant came into my room last night
> and kicked me in the pants.
> My bottom hurt so much I could not sit down
> so I cleaned my room instead.
> My mother was so happy
> She baked me a special cake.
> I guess it is ok to get kicked in the pants
> Every once in awhile.

Prose is even a smaller step. Dreams are, after all, stories in and of themselves, often complete with rising and falling action, climax and subplots. Seldom does a child sit at the desk chewing pencil to pieces for the duration of the writing period when given license to create from a dream. And why even be relegated to a single dream? Episodes from two or three might well make for the most original tale of all.

In doing this form of creative writing, it is best to start with quiet time. This provides the opportunity to go within and re-experience the dream. Once the feeling tone is recaptured along with the vividness of the cast of characters and the plot, then one can write. It may be that the piece of writing will center around the dream in its entirety; in other instances, it may be that the dream provides initial inspiration, but that creative imagination will carry it into quite a different form.

Henry Reed, editor of THE SUNDANCE COMMUNITY DREAM JOURNAL prefaces a section devoted to "Dreams and Creative Writing" (Spring 1977 edition[7]) with the thought that dreams and creative writing are like mutually supportive patrons in that they enrich one another while enhancing growth in consciousness. To explore the potential and implications of this most natural partnership he says, is to learn of the relationship between art and self-healing.

Any time the mind seeks to give birth to an original idea — a work of prose or a new invention — it must first soar beyond inhibitions imposed by conventional logic. Perchance this is why so much original inspiration comes either from dreams or from the very fringes of consciousness, just prior to sleep or full awakening or in a meditative reverie. Originality has small value, however, if it cannot be given meaning in terms of the conscious intellect. Not only must one dream, s/he must articulate those dreams in order to enter into the partnership of which Reed speaks. It is said that intuition/inspiration and intellect are polarized. The former can but "do", the latter can but "know why". Creativity builds the bridge, then the flow begins.

Dance and Dramatization

I asked my dreams one evening to give me some pointers on how to work with children's dreams. I was given a scenario that night: I am passing a dance class and find myself longing to become a participant. My abilities in that regard are nil, so I venture in timidly and seek out the instructor. I tell him I know nothing about dance and am hesitant to try but that something had drawn me in. He encourages me, and suddenly a graceful woman appears who takes me by the arm and leads me onto the dance floor. Together we glide in what to me is sheer ecstasy of movement. It is like the sensation of flying, except my feet never leave the floor.

I shared that dream the next day with the children. At one level I recognized it to contain a personal message about my creative abilities. However, dreams often have several meanings implicit within them, and I saw this one also to be a parable of sorts in the sense of a teaching story. I wanted the young ones to know that many times in real life we assume we are unable to engage in some activity simply because our exposure to it has been minimal. In reality, the only factor limiting us is that insidious four letter word: "can't". What happens when we assume we cannot do something, only to find in a dream we are able to do it rather well? Are we not being shown a side of ourselves that can inspire new confidence such that we learn realistically how to dispute whatever blocks we may have arbitrarily set up for ourselves?

The urging of the dream seemed to have some effect, but the unexpected twist was that the children appeared eager to see if they could be shown dances in their own dreams. We decided to watch dreams carefully that next week and perhaps use a little well-placed auto-suggestion to the effect of receiving dance instruction. The next session, a sparkling seven-year-old who customarily moved about as though she were in tune with an inner rhythmic beat, returned with a dream containing a dance she felt she could share, given a partner. Malea rose to the occasion, and they were excused to the coat room to rehearse the choreography. We set up an impromptu stage, and I was summoned to be given instructions as to how to introduce the performers by their stage names: Lilly Pad and Johnny Strut! What ensued brought down the house. It began as a stylized ballet; however the dreamer ballerina was paired with a partner who heard quite a different beat. Finally a compromise evolved much akin to a flamboyant boogie with others joining in.

Dances, boogie or ballet, need not emerge directly from dream images. Setting a dream to motion becomes a dance form wherein different parts of the dream are taken on by different children. The mood of the dream will set the rhythm of the pace which may go on to include pantomime as part of the performance.

If it appears difficult for children to move to their dreams on cue, begin gently and lead them into the form. Head drums are excellent for sounding out beats. Commence with a slow cadence and have the children walk about the room in pace with the beat. Lighten and quicken the tempo, encouraging them to do likewise. Beat a rhythm and have them pretend they are an animal of their own choosing. Have them emulate its walk. By this time, children are usually quite comfortable with body movement, and when asked to walk like some person or animal from their dream, they can do so with ease. It is an amazing sight to have a classroom of elves, giraffes, monsters, and fairy princesses emerge — to dance, ramble, stalk and glide about.

Once secure with body movement as a means of expression, children can then be shown how to actually speak the dream in gesture and movement much as the Hawaiians tell stories with their dance. Fantasy and imagination can be given full reign in such a design, with very graceful images emerging. Whatever form it may take, the dance is a wonderful way of allowing the child to experience body awareness at several levels.

Dramatizations appear to be a foremost way of expanding the dream, and of special delight to young ones who are a bit more in touch with that theatrical part of make-up than are many adults. Staging plays can be as impromptu and spontaneous as the example presented in the chapter on challenging dreams or as carefully planned and researched as the productions presented in children's theatres. By this I mean using the dream as the inspiration for an actual script and drawing on the symbols for costumes, scenery and props.

Recreating the dream with its case of characters has the added attraction of allowing the dream to be brought to completion. This brings about a closure almost impossible when working analytically with children in formal dream interpretation. Many who have attempted the latter find that children are bored wih the process, perhaps because the dream subjected the cold light of reason has in effect been destroyed. Dramatizations, on the other hand, sustain the vital life and flow which makes the dream so special and intriguing to children. The healthy group interaction which they encourage is a beneficial side effect.

Dream dialogues can be carried out with puppets, but preferably not the kind which are ready-made. The fun way is to use brown paper bags, with the bottom of each bag becoming the frame for faces. Each young dreamer can create figures from his/her dreams on the respective bags. Once accomplished and bag on each hand, dialogue is readily forthcoming. Molly had a monkey conversing with the moon. The monkey was miffed because the moon would not stay a crescent all the time in the sky. It was only as a crescent that Mr. Monkey could hang from it by its tail. When the moon became full, he would slip off. But the moon said that monkeys were not supposed to just hang around all of the time. Productive work was needed too, so as to light the way for tiny night creatures to do their marketing once a month. You may well find you will not need a television around when children are introduced to this form of dream dialogue!

Sculpting Dream Images:

Clay is the most tactile medium of creative expression. It is responsive, slippery, gritty, good for pounding, fun to pinch, to throw and roll. It particularly lends itself to characterizations and special symbols coming from the dream. Like paints or crayons, it provides a way for giving form to at least a portion of the dream from whence one can go on to share more, using the sculpture as a reference point.

For children who have not often used clay, it is wise to let them first spend time familiarizing themselves with it, handling and squeezing it into various free shapes. They can pretend these are gift-wrapped objects and then proceed to trace out with "x-ray vision" what is inside them from the dream. From then on it is a matter of either pulling away the wraps or moulding the outside in such a way it begins to reveal the form of the character they have imagined.

A Potpourri:

In addition to the more commonly used media, there are a host of others which may be touched upon lightly: collages can be fashioned from all sorts of materials upon which dream imagery is portrayed. It could be treated as the honoring of selected dreams. By the same token, images could be chosen which present some special theme which the creator may come to intuit as the collage takes form.

The collage might be ideal for creating a dream shield, reminiscent of the shields of American Indians. Their shields displayed a composite of symbols which had particular relevance to their individual growth patterns. Similarly, dream shields present those dream symbols which in often intuitive ways, seem particularly vivid and profound to the dreamer.

The mandala is a sacred art form found within all cultures. Its totality is a symbol of wholeness, a circular form from whose center-point swirl out configurations of consciousness portrayed in symbols. In actuality, the figure speaks to the process of centering, symbolic of eternal potential from which source all grows, develops and reaches fruition. Children often spontaneously create mandala forms in their art work, emanating as it does from the unconscious process going on within. In the dream shield, the child is encouraged to form a mosaic drawn from symbols surfacing from several dreams, all unified within a circle. The visual rendering of symbols in this form provides a further opportunity for contemplation of the dream, and may well move beyond this into prose, poetry or creative insight.

Photography might lend itself to creative dream work. Arthur Tress's THE DREAM COLLECTOR[8] may serve as a source of inspiration for work in this area. The book is a collection of photographic interpretations of the dreams of a number of children. Tress, a photographer, believes that children's dreams are as important to emotional health as reading, writing and arithmetic. He feels that spontaneous acting out of dramatic situations enhances creative imagination much more than does forced learning.

Tress asked a group of children to record their dreams and then to act them out. Once the child was totally involved in the dramatization, Tress began photographing. The pictures speak for themselves; it is obvious the children thoroughly enjoyed the process. This could easily be adapted to children photographing one another in the midst of dream dramatizations, especially if a unit on photography and dark room use was available.

And how about block prints or printing unique dream symbols on cotton t-shirts for an eye-opener? It is not difficult to find old inner tubing. Symbols can be drawn right on the rubber, cut out easily and glued on a wooden block. A wide collection of fabric dyes are available since so much art decor of fabric is now in fashion; consequently it is not difficult to create dream apparel in a single session, once the materials are assembled.

The imagination knows no bounds when it comes to teaming up with dreams. For ideas of your own, put the question to your own dream self and let fantasy soar. Collaborate with colleagues or other parents, and perhaps best of all, brainstorm with the children themselves.

One word of caution however: it is easy to get involved with the vast potential for creative expression which lies within the dream, to the extent that dreams can be overdone early on. There seems to be a developmental period in working with dreams as with everything else, a process best nurtured slowly until it can blossom in its own time. A child's personal discovery of the value of dream work is far more important than our pushing him/her forward with our knowledge and enthusiasm.

Work of this nature with children can only be done successfully in an atmosphere where trust and caring are the essential components of the group dynamic. The very act of sharing one's inner life fosters healthy acceptance and honest relating. To continue and deepen, underlying empathy and concern for human values must be preserved.

Einstein exalted the experience of the mysterious, declaring it was the fundamental event which forms the cradle of true art and true science. No matter what the method or material selected for creative expression, it is the creative act itself that will beckon forth the mysterious. Supplied with the materials and encouragement, the child is guided towards a goal or value which may well remain secret and inner. Well and good. Like the ancient potter, our concern is not so much with the pot forming between the child's groping hands as with the spirit which speaks in its own mysterious ways to those who listen in silence, then sing its song in the act of creation.

Challenging Dreams

"It wasn't a very long dream, but it was real scarey," said David. "I was sure glad I woke up before I got hurt."

"Can you tell me about it?" I inquired. He nodded, and this is what followed:

There was a big tree. I was standing under it. All of a sudden I knew it was going to fall over, and if it did, it would crush me to pieces. I was so frightened that I started to cry, and then I woke up.

"Dave, why don't you draw a picture of what happened in the dream. Maybe the tree doesn't have to fall. What could you do so it wouldn't?"

Puzzlement, followed by deep thought on the part of the little six-year-old. Then out came the crayons. Five minutes of intense labor followed. Art work completed, a picture was thrust into my hands with a triumphant smile.

"Look, Kathy, at the tree now. I put Christmas tree lights all over it so it is too beautiful to fall down. If it does, it will break all the lights, and it doesn't want to do that."

"David, that is a stroke of genius. What do you think might happen if you had the same dream again?"

"I probably wouldn't cry. I guess I could make it safe by myself. But if the tree was really big, I might put some hooks on it and fasten it to the ground — just to make sure."

A bad dream? On one level. Yet out of it came both ingenuity and a creative form of courage. The wailing voice which first told the dream changed to the voice of a self-confident young man who realized he could take charge of a frightful situation in a very responsible fashion.

For quite some time it has seemed to me that the dreams we call "bad" or "fearsome" should actually better be termed "challenging". Perhaps more than any other classification of dream, these are staged by the psyche precisely so that we can learn a new way of handling life — at least those portions which are proving disruptive at some dimension of being.

It is as though such dreams challenge us to let go of antiquated forms of energy which keep us from being integrated persons. The challenge is met by encountering these productions head on. Honoring their message, difficult though it may be, and learning to work adaptively with them, we attempt to integrate their teaching so that more wholistic patterns of behavior may emerge. Don Juan taught Carlos Castaneda that a warrior (a man or woman of courage and honor) views everything that happens as a challenge, whereas the average person views events as either a blessing or a curse. To see a "bad" dream as a challenge is to accept its teaching for one's greater growth in such a way that its "badness" becomes a cause for celebration rather than fear. The wise consider misfortune or adversity as virtual gifts for our greater understanding. If we apply this philosophical attitude to bothersome dreams, our manner of working with them is radically altered. No longer will we be limited; repressing, belittling, ignoring, or worrying over them.

Some intuitively take such dreams as challenging. Certainly I can attest to adults who have registered for dream classes and workshops precisely because of their "bad" dreams. They may be the only ones recalled, but so potent are they that the individual feels it vital to gain skills for deciphering their content. The psyche works very hard to get our attention, and one sure way of doing that is to stage productions which are so terrifying that we can no longer ignore them.

Challenging dreams are no respecter of age. While children seem to have more than their share of monster dreams, adults have their own variations on the theme. The feature common to all these dreams is that the person, child or adult, is at war in some symbolic way with self. This is another reason why such dreams need to be perceived as challenging. Wars evolve when the natural laws of harmony and balance are violated. Applied to psychic functioning, such violations occur at every level: physical, emotional, mental and spiritual. We are multi-dimensional beings and achieve completion by being in balance with all facets of ourselves.

A personal example will serve to illustrate. Periodically in my dreams I have difficulty with film projectors. I classify these as "bad" because my sense of frustration is so pronounced in them. I thread the film incorrectly or the projector doesn't handle 16 mm films or the audio-visual department sends them at the wrong time. Because I have long since cracked this personal symbol, I now recognize its appearance as an admonition about the subtle intrigues or warrings with my mental body. Inevitably these are times when I quite literally am "projecting". I am taking either the undesirable or unexplored aspects of myself and placing them on others so I can save myself the anxiety of having to look long and hard at disowned parts of myself. In reviewing my behavior of the preceeding day(s), I become aware of some of myself which I have projected. Yet at the time I was totally oblivious, at least at a conscious level. However, at an unconscious level, I apparently am not going to let myself get away with such blindness; hence a frustrating battle ensues so I may continue my work toward personal growth and understanding.

Children fight their own nightly battles with inner concerns. Had I known when I was eight as I do now how to work with personal symbols, would I have been spared my own dream traumas? Probably not. Once again, let me stress one does not work with children's dreams in the same manner as with adults. What eight-year-old could understand the intricacies of the ego defense mechanism of projection, much less look at it in terms of self-application? Besides, comparative content analysis of frightening dreams between adults and children reveals quite differing themes. Let us move then to looking specifically at how one educates the little person for warrior stance since the tremors of battle can be particularly scarring to those more in touch with the inner territory where such struggle is staged.

Probably the key to helping children come to terms with their challenging dreams lies in being able to experience the world of fear much as does the child, and then responding in nurturing and responsible ways which enable the child to both encounter the fear head-on and use it as a point of growth. To this end, it is absolutely critical that we recognize the reality of another person's fear as not gauged by our own attitude toward the object of fear but rather by the attitude of the one who is experiencing the fear. The reality lies with the fear; not with the object. Unless one is able to accept the legitimacy of the fear, it cannot be dealt with in an adaptive, healing fashion.

I know of a mother who was continually frustrated by her daughter's dreams of tigers under her bed. The child would awaken screaming and have to be taken into her parents' bed for the remainder of the night. The mother had tried turning on the lights and showing the child there was nothing of which to be afraid. This was the mistake of relating to the object of the fear, rather than the fear itself. Finally the mother began to get more in touch with adaptive ways of working with fear. One night when the dream was particularly intense, she awakened the little girl, proceeded to reach under the bed and drag forth the animals as the child watched. The mother rushed out the door with them one by one, and in polished theatrical style, slung them down the stairs and out the front door. As she did this, she greatly relieved the child, who for the first time in months went back to sleep in her own bed. On two other occasions, the drama was restaged when the tiger dream presented itself. Thereafter it never returned. The child was three and a half. Obviously there are limitations to this technique imposed by age. But the point is well taken. Once the legitimacy of the fear is acknowledged, it can then be dealt with adaptively.

Quite frequently there is a well-intentioned effort to replace fear with bravery. This takes some form of admonition such as: "You couldn't possibly be afraid of that; you know dinosaurs (or whatever) are non-existent" or "can't hurt you" — depending upon the object of the fear). Yet the stark fact remains that the child is afraid. That fear is undoubtedly quite unintelligible to the child; nonetheless it persists regardless of adult efforts to the contrary.

The end result is often that the child who receives this kind of response feels inadequate and probably will be ashamed to reveal fears in the future. How would an adult feel who perceives some event or person as threat producing when all others in his/her acquaintanceship are totally accepting? Obviously this makes the one so bothered less brave than the others in the group. There are two areas of concern in such a case. First is the threat of the fear itself; secondly, the feelings of inferiority and insecurity which surface in the face of a lack of courage. A child will literally shut its humiliated self away with fears. Frances Wickes amplifies this concept with her formula which states that as the power of fear increases, the sense of competency decreases.[9]

We know there is a strong relationship between feelings of competency and self-confidence. Each nurtures the other. Consequently when competency decreases, a child becomes all the more anxious and unwilling to risk acting in more responsible ways. With the fall into helplessness, the child becomes more withdrawn and dependent upon others for decision-making processes.

A related and equally damaging response to a child's "bad" dream is ridicule. In most cases such ridicule is certainly not cruel in intent; yet the effect can be to heighten the child's concerns. There is an old saying that laughter drives away the devil, but its point of application should not be with children's challenging dreams. Quite the contrary. Rather than decreasing the fear, laughter and ridicule work to undermine the child's own sense of confidence.

Some people laugh at another's folly out of their own anxieties. Ridicule in this case may well derive from feeling helpless to know how to work adaptively with whatever concern is presenting itself. Therefore, all the more reason to explore ways in which the child can be guided so as to rise to the challenge of the fearsome experience.

One of the most responsible ways of working with disturbing events is to admit them openly. A concern can be dealt with only after it is admitted into awareness. Unfortunately the mechanism of "denial" is one of the more common defenses drawn upon when fear raises its head. Psychological naivete fosters the assumption that if we deny the situation, it ceases to exist. A corollary to this is that one can then easily turn his/her back on the problem and escape responsibility for working towards its solution.

How much more growth-producing to admit openly such intangible fears, so as to work towards conquering them. And to foster this pattern, particularly in a child, is to build a sense of competency and confidence which come by gaining mastery over its own fears. Our culture tends to value realities which are tangible, material and externalized. The inner life evolves through symbols and in intricate psychological processes. Since it is unfamiliar territory to most, it is easily disregarded. When one's sense of reality is tuned only to the world of outer fact, fears arising from inner images are all too easily brushed aside as unreal.

Fear of the dark is one of these common worries which surface from inner images. Many parents find it nonsensical and resort to night lights to quell the small one's anxieties. But night lights well may be a band-aid solution, working only with the symptom and not the cause. The child still remains helpless to come to terms with the internal dynamics of the concern, for the help has been externalized in the form of a light, with parents assuming he or she will sooner or later outgrow the fear.

How much more adaptive and reasonable to be able to say to a child: "I know you are afraid of the dark. Many people have this fear also, particularly those who live in forests and have to be careful of wild animals prowling around. It is different for us, though, because we live in a house that is safe." If in truth the parent recalls being frightened of the dark when young, it is wise to share that and speak to the number of adults today who had similar concerns before they understood the fear and took control of it. What this sort of communication does is first accept the fear. The child's attitude is being respected, not ridiculed or deprecated. Secondly, the child is being linked to other brave people who have felt similar fears and who have gone on to conquer them. The fear has been legitimized. Such is absolutely critical if the child is to gain control over it.

As much as fears need to be legitimized when working with children, they also need to be externalized. In that way, rather than the fear manipulating the child, the reverse is effected, with the child learning how to take power over the fear. Take for example the witch who chases a little girl in a dream in an endeavor to catch her in Hansel and Gretel fashion. First I would want to listen to the entirety of the dream, encouraging all the intricacy of detail possible. Therein may lie potential solutions. However, I would not be overtly directive if such solutions appear to present themselves. Rather, I would present them in the form of suggestions or in the form of a query; i.e.: "What might happen if you stopped short in your running from the witch, faced her and demanded to know why she was running after you?"

This might lead into a fantasy dialogue with the witch wherein the child would be encouraged to play one or both roles. At first, my playing the role of the witch might be easier so as to find a positive outcome. Then the roles could be switched, for once the child learns how to orchestrate a positive outcome, she needs to feel its effects directly herself.

If such an approach seems too advanced or if I were to meet with blocking behavior, then I would suggest we converse together about the witch; how we could find out why she likes to chase children, how we could turn her into our friend, what might have happened to her when she was a little girl herself to cause her to grow into a witch rather than a physician/healer.

In the work Caroline Beard DeClerque has done with children and problem dreams, she has found it is best to suggest solutions because the child must first be convinced alternatives to the dream design will be viable ones. But she finds that before too long, a child needs only the stimulus of a few leading questions in order to stimulate imagination. This is indeed the goal for which parent or guide must aim since the child created the original dream and must remain the final authority over what will work.

There are many, many other ways of externalizing the fearsome dream image. It could be painted or sculpted in clay. A story or poem could be written about it. The techniques will vary with the child and his/her special interests. For example, if a child were musically inclined, how auspicious to write a song about the dream character or beat out a rhythm which resonates with the imagery. A particularly innovative suggestion from Caroline DeClerque[10] is to mold the image of the frightening symbol in cookie dough, bake it, and then gain true mastery as it is joyfully ingested!

Another original form of externalization was reported in a case study by Dr. Leonard Handler, a psychotherapist working with an eleven-year-old boy who was so terrified by nightmares of monsters that he could not sleep through the night.[11] After an indication that the boy wanted to work on the problem, Dr. Handler had him climb into his lap. He instructed him to then close his eyes and to pretend the monster was actually in the room with them. Holding the little boy tightly, Dr. Handler pounded his desk and demanded the monster leave immediately, so his little friend would no longer be bothered.

It took a few tries before the child indicated the monster had left. The procedure was then repeated, but this time the young man was encouraged to also pound and shout. Afterward the child was very proud of himself. The next go around was with the lights off; first with Dr. Handler issuing the directives and then with the boy's accompaniment. The child was then asked to repeat this behavior at home. The next week he joyously reported his monster had returned only once and left immediately when the shouting began. By the second week, the nightmares no longer were occurring, and the boy could sleep undisturbed through the night.

Such monster dreams are not isolated examples. Monsters seem to be a common theme in children's dreams. It makes for a very intriguing session when each has the opportunity to share one of his/her own scarey monster dreams. I notice they receive these dreams from one another with great respect. For some, it is undoubtedly a revelation that others share dreams of a similar quality. So many fears are intensified because we mistakenly think we alone have such concerns. To find strength in numbers and an empathic camaraderie is a big step in gaining mastery over these challenges. The next step may be to create a "monster mural" and let the children really get into it with colorful paints. Guaranteed it will be a sight to behold and a topic of conversation for days to come. The exercise may begin with serious overtones but will no doubt conclude with peals of hilarity. Whether the self-same monsters will retain their power is questionable.

I might note that some of these monster escapades I engaged in were with a group of mixed ages, ranging from six to eleven. The younger children were wide-eyed at the dreams of the older ones. By the same token, the older ones were very under-standing and compassionate of the dreams of their younger cohorts.

In one of our sessions, a bright, highly articulate and confident young lady of eleven shared a particularly horrendous monster dream which sent chills down the backs of us all. Following is the dream verbatim:

I dreamed my family and I were in a big house and I was carrying my little brother in my arms. All of a sudden the house started to cave in. Me and my little brother ran out, but he got hit on the head and was dead. I did not know this. Everyone else in the house was crushed. A cop car started coming. They said we would have to go to a home because my parents were dead. I said: "No", and started running with my dead little brother in my arms. We were out in barren wasteland. I looked back and saw instead of policemen in the car, they were demons. They were great big and horrid and all red. I started running and then my

own brother turned into one of those demons. I dropped him and
ran up a tree. They all came up after me and started tearing at me,
so I jumped down. There was a pit below, and it was full of fire. I
jumped in and started to burn up, so I climbed up the sides until I
got to a big pool of ice water and jumped in there. But then a big
monster rose up and started to pull me in. I had a knife that I
reached for and started stabbing him. He was mad, so I got up on
a tree branch and hung there out of his reach. But the branch
broke, and I fell right into his jaws!

We all sat stunned at first, then various children asked her to
elaborate upon certain parts. I suggested we attempt a
dramatization of the dream, and lo and behold, a spontaneous
cast of characters rose to the occasion. A six-year-old became the
baby brother; others became the demons with an active eleven-
year-old becoming the monster. But as the re-enactment began
to unfold, a curious thing happened. Right about the time the
young lady was finding the stabbing pointless and was preparing
to make for the tree, the demons broke script and had an uprising
among themselves, turning on the monster. What a beating the
poor monster took; as a matter of fact, our eleven-year-old actor
was adamant in resolving that he would never assume such a role
again. The young lady was delighted; with her friends to the
rescue, the dream had released its fearsome hold on her. And
needless to say, a lot of energy had been dissipated, for the action
had become intense in places.

Of course when I had suggested a dramatization, I had no idea
what would be the outcome. Nor did the children, for we did not
hold a rehearsal. But children, I have found, have their own kind
of wisdom and whatever collective urge caused them to alter the
script, most assuredly all I could do was applaud and wonder why
I had ever been concerned as to whether I had chosen the right
course of action!

Notice that in each of these episodes where the dream was
externalized, the child did not in any way analyze the fearsome
symbol. This would be just the opposite were we working with
adults, but as noted earlier, such introspection with children,
particularly the younger ones, might well lead to morbid self-

interest. What is far more important is to honor the concern, give it form and encourage the child either to befriend it or take power over it such that it ceases to be the manipulative force it once was.

Also, the freeing act of sharing a challenging dream with an empathic listener is yet another viable approach. Frances Wickes tells of a little girl who had scarey dreams of a green monkey who continually chased her in dreams and finally she told her mother about it.[12] In the telling of the story, she realized she had lost her fear. She asked her mother why that was so. The mother wisely replied that everyone had green monkeys in their heads as well as all sorts of other animals and people that stories were made about, but that some individuals could see them more clearly and more easily than others. Therefore, to tell this to someone who understood about green monkeys but who also was a person who did all the normal daily things such as brushing teeth, eating, exercising, and so on, made the story characters and the real world come together. After that conversation, the child's night terrors ceased. Obviously the mother's skillful handling was the reason why. She made no attempt to deal with the symbolism of the green monkey; rather she handled the fear with a simple explanation which made a dream clothed in mystery much more natural. And by so doing, she paved the way for future confidences.

Children have been reassured when I have spoken of my own challenging dreams to them. Sometimes it has been the catalyst for eliciting their own, which previously they have not wished to admit. So much can be gained from the adaptive attitude toward these types of dreams on the part of the adult. Sometimes I share with them that I have had to learn to become brave to deal with some of my dreams, but that I have grown considerably as a result.

Such a teaching can easily be put in the form of an improvised fairy tale or in mythological terms. In so doing, it often becomes more of a catalyst for modeling. Not even our television generation of children has grown beyond a love of these two age-old modes of instruction. Teaching stories, such as parables and fairy tales, are profound in that they enable the child to make his/her own connections and to draw conclusions based upon their own reasoning abilities. They teach, as it were, from the inside out as opposed to arbitrary dictates from authority figures. In this regard, if a child is frightened by figures from a bad dream which continue to haunt him/her while awake, they can often be explained as self-made fairy tales very much like the people or animals which storytellers saw when they made up their wonderful stories like Jack and the Bean Stalk. At that point, I would undoubtedly encourage the child to sit down with me and fashion our own tale incorporating those dream figures.

Though our emphasis has been on indirect ways of handling the challenges which these dreams imply, there are instances where it is appropriate to probe into the fear itself, given skillful hands and heart. Much will depend on the age of the child and level of comprehension.

I know of a wise grandmother who periodically kept her grandson overnight. One evening an hour after bedtime, he awoke crying and sobbing over a nightly terror involving Star Wars characters. The grandmother knew that something more than movie dramatizations was involved. The boy was very precocious for his eight years, and she explained that the frightening episode represented something that was in real life frightening to him. She took the child into bed with her and gently encouraged him to talk about what was weighing so heavily on his mind. The process took patience and love before the concern came tumbling out. Together they turned it over and over, seeking to understand its ramifications. It involved a third party, so they agreed together to talk with the one so involved. The next day, the matter was brought out in full light, with grandmother providing moral support and communication skills. Clarifications were forthcoming, along with necessary assurances. A mighty weight was removed from the small shoulders, and thereafter the child slept peacefully.

There will always be those times when such an approach is the appropriate one. A caution however: adults need always to be careful to do too little instead of too much in dealing with the unconscious material of a child. We may have our own theory about what causes the concern, but the dream life of that child should never be dissected simply to verify our own suppositions. If it is not possible to get a simple statement of the concern from the child which verifies our intuitive sense, it is much wiser to cease the probe immediately and opt for a less direct plan of action. This is particularly true for educators who are not usually in such close rapport with the child as to know the intricacies of very personal situations.

It will thus be seen that creative empathy and loving concern remain the most essential tools for working with challenging dreams. Whatever approach one may elect to take as these dreams surface, it will only be successful when coupled with an attitude of compassionate understanding and respect. And that attitude will always be found to rest on the bedrock of trust and love; a foundation which inevitably will give the child strength to rise to the challenges presented by this form of dream.

"Psi" Dreams

 "Wanna hear a miracle story?" inquired Andrew as we sat on the floor talking about unusual dreams. Miracles did not cease after Galilee, I feel, and I found myself ready and willing. The children, eager as usual, seem unusually close to such events.

My mom had a special dinner for dad and me one night. After a neat apple pie, she announced I was going to have a little brother or sister in about seven months. That night I dreamed it wasn't one little brother, but that two baby sisters were coming. I told mother the next morning about the dream, and she just smiled. About a month later she came home real puzzled and said the doctor for the first time had heard two heart beats. She said the dream was right after all because there were going to be twins in our family. And when they finally arrived — guess what? Two baby sisters!

A miracle or a precognitive experience? Choose your label as you wish; more important than the label is the event itself. Precognitive, clairvoyant and telepathic experiences form a phenomenon collectively known as "psi", a term having reference to a type of energy often classified as our sixth sense.

The notion of E.S.P. or "extra sensory perception" is now falling more and more into disuse since these phenomena are no longer really seen as something "extra" or outside ourselves, available only to a select few. In reality, probably most of us to some degree possess these abilities; the question is to what extent and how cognizant an individual is of their presence. As growing numbers of people report psi experiences, what is paranormal is no longer thought to be "abnormal". Further, it is obvious there is a growing interest and acceptance of psi over the last few years.

What can be said about such energies in a collective sense? First and foremost that they function in a most elusive manner. To try and pin them down is akin to attempting to hold the wind in an embrace. There is no question but that one experiences the caress of a breeze, but to feel its form and outline is nigh impossible. Yet, evasive as the quality of psi may be, its underlying characteristic remains an intermittent realization of some form of consciousness occurring outside the reaches of the ordinary senses. In telepathy one becomes aware of the thoughts of another without any of the usual senses being the instigator of the impression. Clairvoyance is the acquisition of information about inanimate objects such as the contents of an unopened letter. It can also be an awareness of an event taking place concurrently with the thought form, such as an awareness of the death of a loved one at the actual moment of passing. As with telepathy, that awareness does not arise from the cues of any of the senses. In precognition an individual receives awareness of future events or of those past. An important feature common to all three is that the cognitions are totally independent of space and time; i.e. a precognitive dream of a future event in some distant land or a telepathic exchange bridging thousands of miles. Further, the thoughts or experiences cover a whole gamut from the most trivial of encounters to others momentous in scope.

Anyone who has studied his or her dreams and has shared them with others is no newcomer to psi. As a matter of fact, parapsychologists are quite adamant in affirming dreams as the safest way to gain first-hand experience with these abilities. That psi exists, both within the dream and within waking consciousness

I can attest, along with thousands who speak from their own experiences. How it works is much more difficult to delineate. And this is precisely why parapsychology for so long remained a teasing embarrassment to the discipline of psychology. It is difficult, if not impossible in most cases, to replicate experiments and extract measurable statistical information, the bedrock of the scientific method. And only such data allows reason and logic to scrutinize facts and affirm or deny legitimacy.

Fortunately there will always be researchers who attempt the impossible, and often it is their own kind of prophetic vision (and unwillingness to abide by conventional logic and prevailing sentiment) which advances knowledge to its next step. To that end, Dr. Stanley Krippner and Dr. Montague Ullman have done momentous work in their dream laboratory at New York City's Maimonides Medical Center Psychiatric Department. So extensive is their data and so precise their studies in keeping with scientific methodology, that the individual who stubbornly negates the workings of psi can only be seen as uninformed. Even the most skeptical who reads DREAM TELEPATHY[13] will be forced to admit to the existence of a fascinating form of energy which transcends that available to our customary senses.

Dreams can be very complex, their symbolism intricate. Only well planned experiments rigorously designed and executed provide data so needed to break through the wall of scientific skepticism regarding the supernormal. Ullman's and Krippner's work presents historical surveys of dream studies and provides an account of their own detailed experimental methodology. Over a hundred studies follow which combine exacting methods of electrophysiology with the dreams of subjects. In reading such material, one becomes increasingly impressed with the great skill necessary to study the complex psychological energies of the unconscious mind in the experimental, quantitative methods of the scientific laboratory. And yet, such careful work is mandatory if parapsychology and psi phenomena are to be elevated from the realm of the "absurd" to their rightful place as an integral, though often latent, part of our being.

There are numerous resources on this general subject of the paranormal. I mention DREAM TELEPATHY because young people bring through a considerable amount of telepathic and precognitive material. I have known children who take such dreams as a matter of course. Others find such dreams quite disturbing, since the phenomenon could not be explained either by parents or by others. A little one may dream of a pleasant occurrence that later manifests. But if one dreams of an accident or some other unpleasant event only to have it come about in literal form, and there is no forthcoming explanation, the child may well choose to repress dream recall from this point forward. It may appear to the child that the dream was, in some mysterious way, the cause of the event.

For this reason it is wise for parents and educators to have some understanding of the workings of psi. Obviously this may be demanding because of its elusive nature. But after familiarizing oneself with the literature and when possible, tuning into one's own abilities at an experiential level, it may be much easier to explain psi happenings to a child in common sense terms. What we need to avoid at all costs is surrounding the psychic occurrence with mystical overtones which make it appear even more strange and to be experienced only by those who border on the neurotic.

In taking a common sense approach, it can be of use to learn of the experiences of historical and well-known figures noted for their psychic experiences. This is part of the dream lore spoken of earlier which helps legitimize dreams for children. Abraham Lincoln had a great interest in psychic phenomena, as well as a great respect for his own precognitive dreams. Prior to the battles of Gettysburg and Antietam, Lincoln's dreams portrayed damaged Confederate ships being pursued by Union vessels. Later he had a dream that foretold his own assassination and death.[14] Joseph's dream in Genesis creates deep resonance with young precognitive dreamers; similarly the precognitive dreams of the American Indians and shamans are documented in the literature of anthropology.

It may be of interest for older children to know that precognitive dreams are so prevalent that there are now three dream registries where one can send dreams which appear to foretell a coming event of possible consequence for many persons.

Ben has dreams of both earthquakes and floods, and he describes in great detail what happens to the landscape and to the people involved. He was relieved to discover that people the world over are having what are referred to as "cataclysmic dreams" which portend natural disasters. Ben's dreams may possibly simply reflect certain interpersonal fears and anxieties on his part. But the fact is that Ben is a competent and creative young person and very self-aware for his eleven years. Knowing that others had similar experiences was reassuring to him. Since the nature of those dreams was so inexplicable to him, some repression of dreams had already commenced.

These dream registries are located in New York, London and Toronto.[15] The London registry was a direct outgrowth of the many documented psychic precognitions (both through dreams and premonitions) which foretold the disaster at Aberfan. Aberfan, in Wales, was the site of a massive coal slide in 1966. The catastrophe engulfed the Welsh mining village and took 144 lives, mostly those of school children. The underlying rationale for these registries is that such disaster might be prevented through the recognition of psychic dream warnings. Most who work with the paranormal are well aware that prophecy need not come true; it may be only a question of the alteration of energy forms once the danger has been recognized.

Since these registries are staffed by volunteers, it is not always possible at present to systematically review and catalogue all material received so as to ascertain the possible scope of the event which several dreams may foretell. And would the public choose to act on the basis of the dream? Perhaps not, but it is significant that such registries do exist. They provide a link among the many dreamers who give serious consideration to their own precognitive material.

Awareness is always step one in growth toward understanding. And that, to me, is the real goal when encountering sensitive young persons who otherwise may repress natural abilities. The principal concern should be to take a balanced and responsible approach toward whatever psychic abilities may surface in the child — whether through dreams, conscious premonitions, or telepathic encounters. Adults may profess disinterest in an attempt to discredit a reality that is perhaps bothersome to them. They may, on the other hand, become overzealous in their attempt to encourage the child to force whatever abilities are evidencing themselves.

Samuel Young in PSYCHIC CHILDREN[16], speaks of situations where children have consciously chosen to stifle psychic impressions because the parent displayed excessive pride in what to the child were natural God-given abilities. By the same token, such ardent attention may cause the child to suspect that parental approval is conditional, that his or her worth is determined by the ability to perform psychic feats. Conditional acceptance implies "I love you for what you do, not what you are," and is a major factor contributing to lack of self-esteem on the part of a child.

Such examples speak of extremes. They contain a message, however, for parents and educators alike. If excessive attention is paid to psychism, a child may equate the phenomenon with performance. The expectation may result that one must give demonstrable evidence on cue. In reality, nothing more inhibits intuition or psi abilities than a heightened self-consciousness. What is natural flows of its own accord. Any attempt to force its occurrence for a waiting audience inevitably meets with failure.

Far better simply to listen to the child who wishes to share psi incidents. If reassurances are needed, then let them be matter-of-fact. Likewise, any other explanatory material should be presented with an eye to its educational value for the particular age and level of sophistication of the child.

With an older group of children, it was possible to conduct telepathic dream experiments. These were children who already had considerable knowledge of psi happenings and who accepted their own precognitive dreams as a matter of course. Marcella and I, for example, undertook to see if we could communicate through dreams. Rather than replicate an experiment where specific images were used, we simply decided to go to sleep in the awareness that we would communicate with one another during the night, and would, on awakening, remember the communication.

Although my dream was hazy, it indicated that either she was to be of help to me or that I was to be of help to her. Slightly puzzled, I was fascinated to hear Marcella's account of our encounter. In her dream she was with another friend, but the over-riding concern was with problems she was having with her parents. In a second episode, she and I discussed the problem, and she gained some insight into how to work it through. Upon awakening, she knew the matter had not yet righted itself. But in sharing the dream later, together we gained a realization as to how it could be handled adaptively. As it turned out, not only was I of help to Marcella, but she was of help to me. Our sharing of the dream gave me cause for reflection.

For some time I have been strongly convinced that dreams serve many levels of communication. Often a matter seems too private, too personal to discuss with another. There is the risk that one will not be understood or that an observation will be misconstrued. In dreams, however, such subjective materials are given form and a theme which facilitate dialogue. Marcella, for example, had apparently been concerned for some while with her problem. Whether she would have shared it with me spontaneously is questionable, and there might have been no way I could give her an answer without belittling her own abilities to work toward a responsible solution. When the dream was shared and examined from different angles, however, it was not long before insights began to surface in Marcella as to how she might work toward resolution of the conflict.

It is not our strengths which bind us together in mutual caring so much as our weaknesses and our needs. Could this partially explain the telepathic or precognitive rapport we have in times of need with those close to us? We know that the psychic life of family members is closely linked, as well as that between close friends.

Children seem particularly adept at intuiting mind states in parents. As a result, what often appears as a "challenging" dream may be the child's portrayal of a parental concern. This points to yet another reason why formal dream analysis is inappropriate for children. Of what possible value could it be to probe into the child's anxiety-producing dream when the responsibility for the problem's solution lies elsewhere?

In Andrea's dream, a mother and father robin are stealthily dismantling their nest, leaving the baby bird exposed and precarious. Andrea is not consciously aware that her parents are planning a divorce. However, the dream stands as clear evidence that the parents' decision is affecting Andrea at psychic levels.

In Andrea's case, two possible courses of action appear: 1) Endeavor to determine if the parents will be more open with her, explaining to them the message of the dream; 2) Allow Andrea to externalize the dream in some form so that she may gain control over the situation symbolically represented.

To attempt to interpret the dream openly to the child would be to place a heavy burden upon her shoulders. Further, such an interpretation might be detrimental to the mysterious process by which the situation is working itself out in the psyche. Many who work with their dreams recognize that the dream process is mysterious and may well effect its own transformation even when not consciously recalled.

Our responsibility is to listen carefully when a young one volunteers a dream and to be sensitive to what the dream may be saying about needs expressed. If the child chooses to work further with the dream, all possible encouragement should be given. But if the child is reticent either to discuss the dream or give it some creative form, then we must accept that decision. Trust and confidence in the process assure us that the resolution will come in other ways.

There is much we do not know about paranormal phenomena. Anyone who works in this field will readily admit that we are still in the kindergarten stage in our attempts to comprehend these particular forms of energy. It is understandable then that those new to the subject of telepathy, precognition and clairvoyance in dreams may have some reservations. With the actual experience of such an event, however, one's regard for the subject is radically changed. For adults, that first experience may well be a vicarious one, coming through the dream of a child. If such is the case, help the child come to terms with it, even if it means recognizing that we can not yet explain the inexplicable. That leap of faith is not so difficult for the child's mind. And it may well be that leap which will intensify the quality of trust so necessary for communing with the inner world.

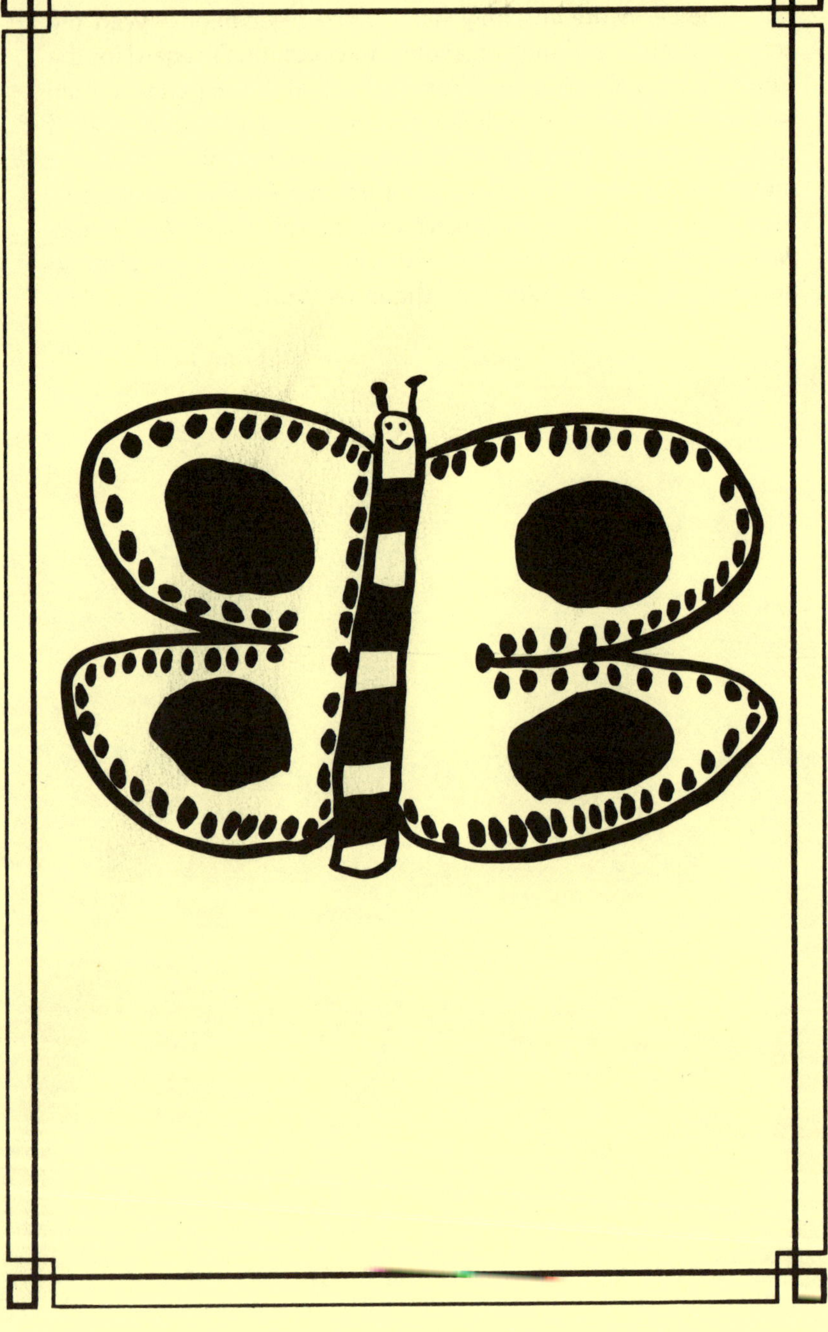

Deputizing Children

One evening I dream I am with my nephew Gordon. I inquire if he would like to come and see my stamp collection. He joyfully agrees. We walk excitedly into my bedroom, eager to look at what I have assembled. Gordon suddenly becomes very quiet, and taking my hand, he points to a butterfly poised upon the cover of the stamp album. As we look more closely, we see it is a most miraculous kind. Although it has glorious wings of many hues, its body is that of a small human form. There is head, body, and legs. Its hands are delicately attached to its wings. We stand in awe, watching it.

I awaken and immediately think of the many butterflies I have seen children draw spontaneously. The butterfly is an ancient and traditional symbol of transformation and transfiguration. I realize that for many years I have seen children more as chrysalises than butterflies. I would look at them and marvel that within lay all the abilities, proclivities, interests and emotions which one day would manifest in adult form. I regarded the task of the parent/teacher/guide as one of drawing forth these inner potentials so the child could come more fully to express its unique design during the period of transformation.

As I come to work more with children, however, I begin to question such a philosophic orientation. Besides, children seldom draw cocoons or caterpillars. Their butterflies are quite mature, yet each very special and splendid in its own color and configuration, be the artist age six or eleven. Every so often in the midst of talking about, painting or acting out dreams with the youngsters, a curious juxtaposition takes place. It becomes difficult to separate the children from the glorious butterflies they draw.

My dream helps me to realize children are not at all in chrysalis stage but instead are already full-fledged butterflies. It is all a matter of perception. As long as I choose to perceive youngsters in chrysalis form, then I remain their mentor, coaxing them to spin a silk of my design and expectation. But as my vision clears, I increasingly see children as quite mature and seek more to listen to that which has already issued forth from pupa stage. Then one night, as if to strengthen that growing conviction comes this dream:

> Fall term begins. Once again I am teaching my graduate course for educators entitled: "Enhancing Creativity in Children through Dream Interpretation." I assign the project which is to build a curriculum around dreams relative to the respective student populations of class members. A teacher in the group vehemently protests and says: "Why not deputize the children and let them create their own curriculum? After all, they are the real authorities."

I awaken laughing, thinking about classroom episodes with young "deputies" whose authority far exceeded the limits of my own when it came to dream application and innovation.

I recall the time I went into a class to demonstrate how to fashion puppets from dream images and conduct dialogues with them. To my surprise, the children turned out to be polished puppeteers of first rank whose artistic and performing puppets made my demonstration seem amateurish by comparison.

I think about my pedantic instructions for dream dramatizations whereas instead, the children without cue inevitably stage spontaneous productions when their dreams seem to so warrant.

With each dramatization they aptly reveal why no director is needed to issue script.

I reflect upon my audacity in actually thinking I can enhance creativity by encouraging children to work with their dreams, when in reality their dream stories, poetry, murals and artistry make it clear they are brimming with creative talent. It is not a matter of "enhancing"; rather that of providing the time, space and encouragement for such creativity to be expressed.

My head reels with these images and more, but then my group of fourth graders comes to mind. They always speak about "dreamouts", defining them as "fairyday ficflies". They tell me that every so often you are given one that is a fluklefuke butterflare. Follow that dreamout with excitagination, they tell me, for its wisdains can never be found in books or in classrooms.

Their understanding and faith give me courage. Somewhere inside, I, too, have a butterfly. Joie even tells me the wings are commencing to unfurl. She says I should stay around children and deputize my own inner child if I wish to see emerge the full promise of wing span, design and decor. I do not have much choice. Joie and fourth graders make a conviving teamata when it comes to my growth and raison d'etre.

So I am off now, scouting for more teachers to teach how to swim. Undoubtedly I shall find another bevilish bunch, excited by dreamas and dreamouts, ficflies and psychowheres. I would ask you to join us, but I suspect time is better spent with your own butterflares and those of your wisdain childbiggers. Well and good. That is the wonder of inakook conversanes. I shall look for you instead some spring morning on a yellow buttercup.

REFERENCES

1. West, Katherine: NEPTUNE'S PLUMMET, A Guidebook for Dreamers. Amata Graphics, 1977

2. Warner, Sylvia Ashton: TEACHER. Simon & Schuster, 1963

3. West, Katherine: NEPTUNE'S PLUMMET, A Guidebook for Dreamers. Amata Graphics, 1977

4. Richards, M.C.: CENTERING. Wesleyan University Press, 1962

5. Spangler, David: FESTIVALS IN THE NEW AGE. The Findhorn Foundation, 1975

6. Koch, Kenneth: WISHES, LIES AND DREAMS — TEACHING POETRY TO CHILDREN. Vintage Press, 1970

7. "Dreams and Creative Writing" in SUNDANCE COMMUNITY DREAM JOURNAL, Spring 1977, p. 220

8. Tress, Arthur: THE DREAM COLLECTOR. Avon, 1972

9. Wickes, Frances: THE INNER WORLD OF CHILDHOOD. Out of print.

10. DeClerque, Caroline Beard: "Dream On; Educating Children to Use Dreams", in SUNDANCE COMMUNITY DREAM JOURNAL, Winter 1978, pp. 62-70

11. Handler, Leonard: "Helping Children with Nightmares", in SUNDANCE COMMUNITY DREAM JOURNAL, Winter 1978, pp. 70-71

12. Wickes, Frances: THE INNER WORLD OF CHILDHOOD. Out of print.

13. Ullman & Krippner: DREAM TELEPATHY. McMillan, 1973

14. "Precognitive Dreaming" in SUNDANCE COMMUNITY DREAM JOURNAL, Summer 1978, p. 174

15. Ibid. pp. 176-8

16. Young, Samuel: PSYCHIC CHILDREN. Doubleday, 1977

UNDERSTANDING YOUR DREAMS

by

Katherine L. West

This is a booklet especially prepared for those who are interested in learning more about the physiology and psychology of the dream state. Both topics are addressed in detail.

Also included are historical antecedents, an emphasis on the rationale for dream work in educational settings, suggestions for interpretative work with adult dreams, and an extensive bibliography.

Available only by mail order for $2.00 from:

AMATA GRAPHICS
17937 S.W. Kelok
Lake Oswego, Oregon 97034

Also available by mail or in fine bookstores:

NEPTUNE'S PLUMMET
A Guidebook for Dreamers

by

Katherine L. West

MYSTICAL	in its depth of vision
MYTHOLOGICAL	in its historical aspects
ASTROLOGICAL	in its design
SYMBOLICAL	in its language of the unconscious
PRACTICAL	in its explication of the process of dream interpretation

Cost: $3.70 including postage
from Amata Graphics